Arts and Cr...

Around the World

Heather Leonard

Acknowledgements

Photos

Tony Stone Images/David Tejada, cover. Tony Stone Images/Oliver Benn, page 6. Werner Forman Archive/Smithsonian Institution, page 8. The Hutchison Library, page 10. Michael Holford, page 12. Werner Forman Archive, page 14. Tony Stone Images/Penny Tweedie, page 16. Bruce Coleman Ltd/Neil McAllister, page 18. ZEFA, page 20. All other photographs by Rupert Horrox.

Text for pages 16 to 17 by Penny Stevenson.
Hand modelling by Lisa Melotti.

Heinemann Educational Publishers
Halley Court, Jordan Hill, Oxford OX2 8EJ
a division of Reed Educational & Professional Publishing Ltd

OXFORD FLORENCE PRAGUE MADRID ATHENS
MELBOURNE AUCKLAND KUALA LUMPUR SINGAPORE TOKYO
IBADAN NAIROBI KAMPALA JOHANNESBURG GABORONE
PORTSMOUTH NH (USA) CHICAGO MEXICO CITY SAO PAULO

© Reed Educational & Professional Publishing Ltd 1997

First published 1997

02 01 00 99 98 97

10 9 8 7 6 5 4 3 2 1

British Library Cataloguing in Publication Data
A catalogue record for this book is available from the British Library.

ISBN 0 435 09571 4   *Arts and Crafts Around the World* individual
                      copy pack: 6 copies of 1 title
ISBN 0 435 09416 5   Stage F pack: 1 each of 7 titles

All rights reserved. No part of this publication may be reproduced or transmitted in any form by any means, electronic or mechanical, including photocopy, recording or any information storage and retrieval system without permission in writing from the publishers.

Colour reproduction by Reacta Graphics.

Printed and bound in Great Britain by Scotprint.

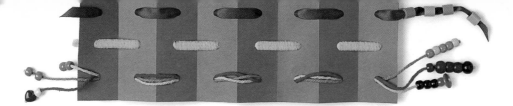

Contents

Arts and crafts around the world

There are many different types of arts and crafts. A craft is a skill which people can learn. It is often useful or decorative, like making a pot or dyeing cloth. Art is a way of telling people our ideas, thoughts and feelings, like making paintings or telling stories with puppets. This book tells you about eight different types of arts and crafts.

People do different types of arts and crafts in different parts of the world. This book tells you where in the world you might find someone doing each type of art and craft. Most of them are practised in other parts of the world too.

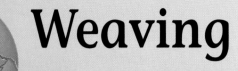

Weaving

A woman weaving fabric in South America

Weaving is lacing threads together. The threads go under and over each other to form a pattern. The woven threads make a fabric or cloth. The fabric can be used for clothing or decoration.

How you can do it

You will need: A4 thin card, hole punch, ribbon, string, wool, paper strips, beads, buttons, shells.

1 Fold the card five times, like a fan.

2 Use the hole punch to make holes along the middle of the paper.

3 Unfold the card and weave ribbon, string, wool or paper strips through the holes.

4 Hang some beads, buttons or shells on the ends.

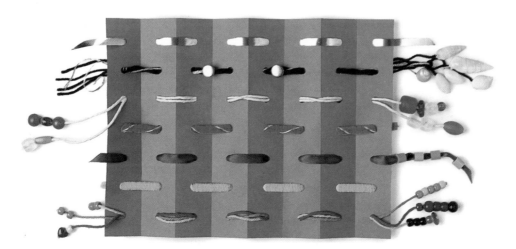

Masks

A Native Alaskan mask

Masks are pictures of animals, people or gods. People wear them over their faces. Some masks are worn to celebrate special occasions. Some masks are used to tell stories. They can be decorated with lots of things.

How you can do it

You will need: pencil, cardboard, scissors, sticky tape, long stick, glue, feathers, seeds, leaves, beads, buttons.

1 Draw a large circle on a piece of cardboard and cut it out.

2 Carefully make two small holes in the cardboard for the eyes.

3 Tape a long stick to the back of the cardboard, half way down.

4 Decorate your mask.

Dyeing

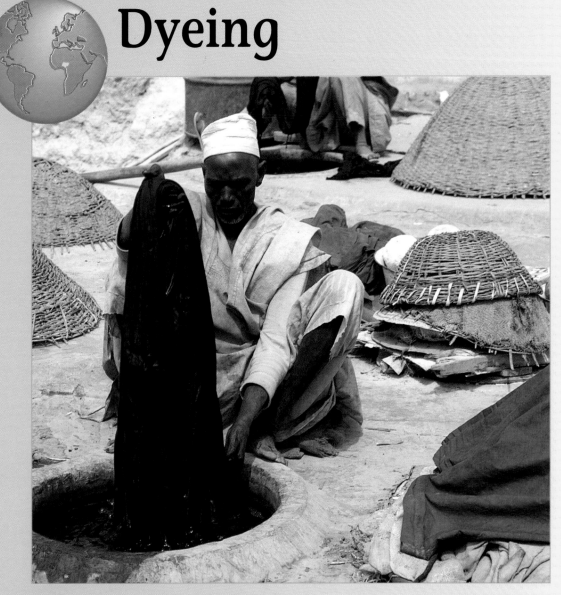

A man dyeing fabric in Nigeria

Dyeing is staining fabric with colours. Fabric is dipped in a coloured liquid. The liquid is called a dye. Some dyes are made from plants. The dyed fabric can be used to make clothing.

How you can do it

You will need: *apron, newspaper, tissue paper, 2 different food colourings, water, 2 bowls.*

1 Add a drop of food colouring to each of the bowls of water.

2 Fold the tissue paper in half, then in half three more times.

3 Dip the corners of the folded paper into the bowls of water.

4 Leave the paper to dry and then unfold it to see the pattern.

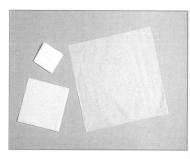

Patchwork

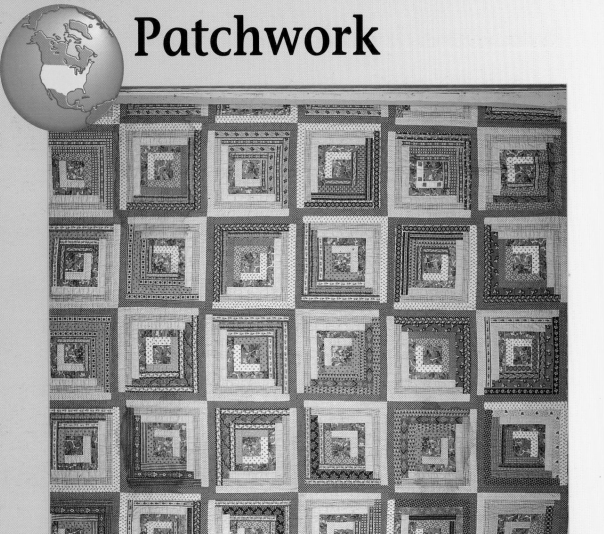

A patchwork quilt from the United States

A patchwork is made by sewing lots of small pieces of fabric together. The small pieces are different colours and patterns. Some patchworks are made into bed covers, called quilts.

How you can do it

You will need: *some old pieces of fabric, scissors, glue, buttons, beads, ribbons.*

1 Carefully cut the pieces of fabric into small squares, all the same size.

2 Glue the squares onto a larger piece of fabric to make one large patchwork.

3 Decorate your finished patchwork.

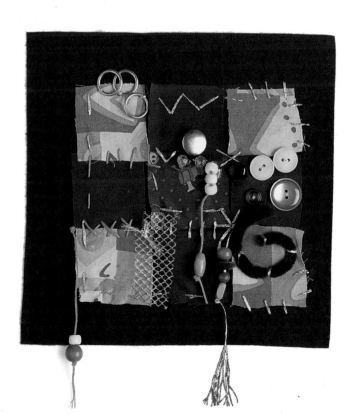

Puppets

A puppet show in Java

Some puppets are 3-D images of people or animals which are moved by hand. They can be used to tell stories. They can be held and moved with sticks. Some puppets can make shadows on a screen.

How you can do it

You will need: *pencil, card, scissors, paper fastener, sticky tape, 2 long sticks.*

1 Draw a simple animal shape.

2 Choose which piece of the animal you want to move. This could be the head or tail.

3 Draw the two parts separately on a piece of card.

4 Cut them out and use a paper fastener to join the two parts together.

5 Tape a stick to the back of each part.

Bark painting

A man painting on bark in Australia

Australian Aborigines paint patterns on bark
cut from trees. They paint with red, brown
and yellow dyes, made out of earth. They also
use charcoal (burnt wood) and white clay.
Most of their pictures tell stories.

How you can do it

You will need: black paper, red, brown, yellow and white pastels, chalks or crayons.

1 Use a piece of black paper instead of bark.

2 Draw patterns of lines and dots on the black paper, using the pastels, chalks or crayons.

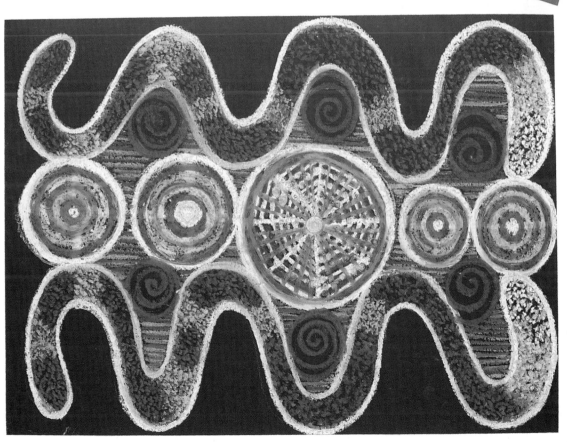

Printing

A man block printing fabric in India

Printing is pressing a stamp onto fabric or paper. Patterns are cut into pieces of wood or rubber. This makes a stamp. The stamp is dipped into ink. It is then pressed onto fabric or paper.

How you can do it

You will need: *apron, newspaper, scissors, sponge, paint, saucers.*

1. Cut the sponge into different shapes.

2. Pour some paint into the saucers.

3. Press the sponge into the paint.

4. Press the sponge onto the paper. You can make lots of patterns using different shapes and colours.

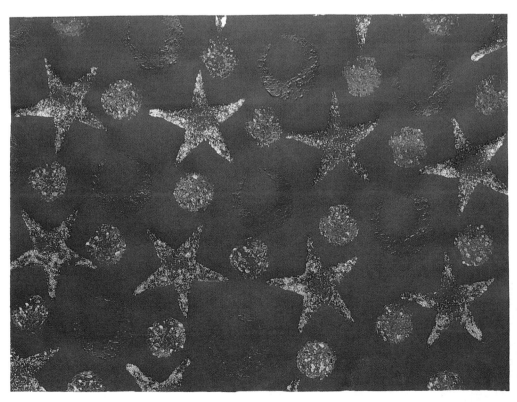

Origami

Origami cranes from Japan

Origami is folding paper into objects or shapes. The paper is not cut or glued.

How you can do it

You will need: *paper.*

1 Fold a square of paper diagonally in half.

2 Follow the folds shown in the pictures.

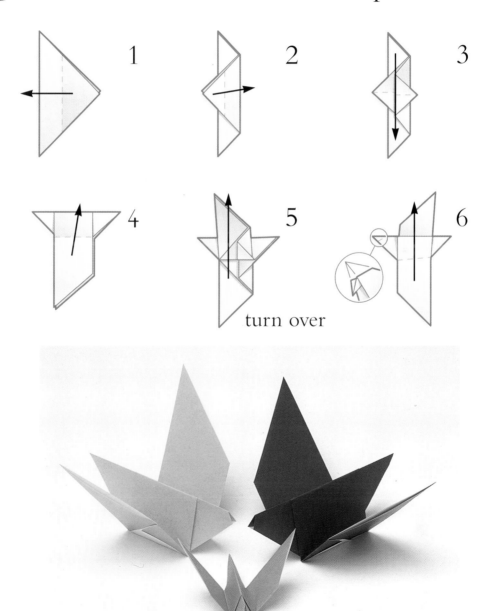

1

2

3

4

5

turn over

6

Arts and crafts chart

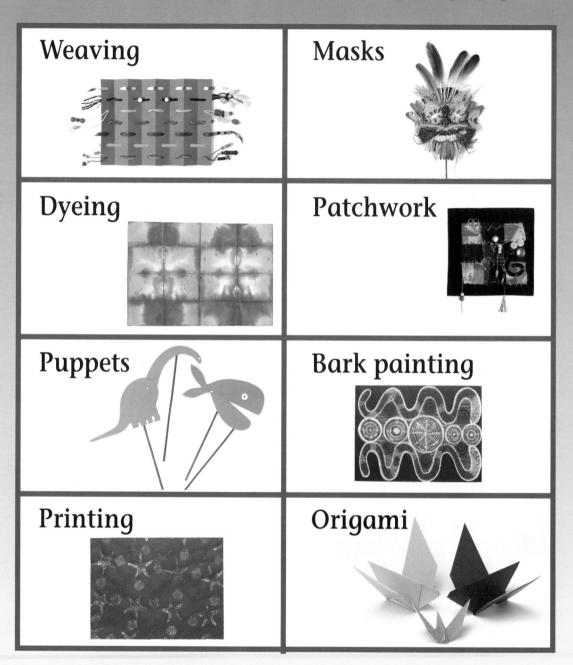

Weaving	Masks
Dyeing	Patchwork
Puppets	Bark painting
Printing	Origami

This chart shows the different sorts of arts and crafts in this book. Can you remember where in the world they are practised? What other types of arts and crafts can you think of?

Further reading

A Child's Book of Art by Lucy Micklethwait,
Dorling Kindersley ISBN 0 7513-5070 2

First Arts and Crafts by Sue Stock,
Wayland ISBN 0 7502 1011 7

Fresh Start (Printing) by Hilary Devonshire,
Franklin Watts ISBN 0 86313 708 3

Making Pictures: Amazing Animals by Penny King
and Clare Roundhill,
Heinemann ISBN 0 600 58289 2

Masquerade: Crazy Creatures by Jacqueline Russon,
Heinemann ISBN 0 431 03587 3

You can also visit your local art gallery
to find out more about arts and crafts.

Index

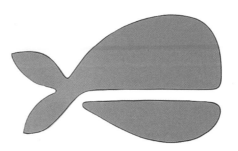